PRESENCES
A Text for Marisol

By Robert Creeley

Presences
A Day Book
Pieces
Words
The Gold Diggers
The Island
For Love

Contexts of Poetry
A Quick Graph
The Charm

PRESENCES

Robert Creeley

Marisol

Charles Scribner's Sons · New York

Grateful acknowledgement is made to the following publications in which some of this material first appeared: *Big Sky, Fiction, Io, Spring Creek,* and *This.* Especial thanks is given to William Katz—who first thought of this book as a possibility, who kept it together throughout its composition, and who finally took on the labor of its design and saw it into press. Without him—nothing.

Copyright © 1976 Robert Creeley

Library of Congress Cataloging in Publication Data
Creeley, Robert, 1926–
    Presences.
    I. Marisol, 1930–   II. Title.
PS3505.R43P7   811'.5'4   75-45211
ISBN 0-684-14364-X

1 3 5 7 9 11 13 15 17 19 V/C 20 18 16 14 12 10 8 6 4 2

Printed in the United States of America

The cover shows *Love,* 1962. 12 x 5 x 4″. The Museum of Modern Art, New York. Photograph by Bevan Davies.

Classicism is based on presence. It does not consider that it has come or that it will go away; it merely proposes to be there where it is.

Donald Sutherland

PRESENCES

1•2•3
2•3•1
3•1•2
1•2•3
2•3•1

1·2·3

One

Big things. And little things. The weight, the lightness of it. The place it takes. Walking around, it comes forward, or to the side, or sides, or backward, on a foot, on feet, on several feet.

There is a top, and a bottom. From the one to the other may be a distance. Equally it may be so dense, or vaporous, so tangential to touch, that an inextricable time passes in the simplest way. If it were to fall, either over, or up, or down, what spaces were there to accomplish would be of necessity measured later. Time runs to keep up, in other words. Already days have apparently gone by in the presence of one.

This is the first time he has spoken in some time, in weeks, in fact. The mouth was, or had been in the sense of what was seen, sealed over with some sort of substance, waxy in look, and, touching it, the feeling was of something sticky, as sticky rubber or sticky gum. This substance, translucent, made the lips seem preternaturally large. Very, very large. To which a footnote: *"He bore a preternatural resemblance to his caricatures in the evening newspapers."* (Evelyn Waugh). But his lips had been sealed. Sealing wax then. Had not someone, possessed of a stamp describing an intricate sphinx, therein and on imprinted that image, on his lips? A cruel, thoughtless joke possibly. The person who did this one thinks of as caring little for others. It must have been an evening, when this occurred. There was nothing else to do insofar as the day had come to nothing. It was rainy, a little chill to the air. One wanted the sun, the sun. There was a beach. Small figures at one far end of it, never quite clear in their detail. Somewhat clifflike rocks surrounded. High above, there seemed to be an open space, which might have been the sky, and yet, in the inexorably close weather, it had to be assumed. Top and bottom, the world?

What was he doing on the beach? No, it was a chair he sat in. He continued to sit in the chair. As if he had been thrown there. He had been thrown there. His small, unobtrusive body lay crumpled against one of the arm rests and his eyes, photographic blurs of grey, were pleading, mutely. In a book of the same order, so to speak, of the ungenerous kinds of people who do not love but nonetheless expect to be loved. Why was he forsaken. He was not. He was placed, in a place. She picked him up and threw him into another place. His little seersucker coat tightly hugged the space under his arms, his armpits, and his diminutive body became rumpled with the impact of being elsewhere. His tie, however, fell straight, undisturbed. Always the gentleman. Being alive, she felt contempt but moved away from it to get some ice from the refrigerator. This, as one says, she put into glasses which she then filled with gin.

The glass was very large. The ice cubes were huge blocks of solidified water.

•

X spoke of having been wakened by sirens toward the middle of the night. Then assumed the police were abroad. In a town of eight hundred people, at midnight, so that they might be coerced into subservience and made to comply with the police imagination of a decent order. Awful. Y wrings hands and wonders why, why. There is, was, a full moon. Perhaps that is why the police have chosen that night? Later Z tells story of being roused at five to answer fire alarm and when they got there, find empty house now gutted with flames, and they are helpless to do more than water down the outbuildings, the barns, and watch the house burn into the rosy dawn. Z lifts the bottle, to drink, and becomes, langorously, the sucking, lips smoothed over the nozzle. The nuzzle. The puzzle. The police.

In a free country, in a country where police enter the imagination as free, free agents, their uniforms are very blue and their badges very large and silver. They make a glittering array, formally. From any point not occupied by them, we see, as few, or others, or many. They may be the same. It is their way of dress that disarms that which stands as us. They can't stand us? Nobody comes, having none. Z recalls Wrentham, Massachusetts at the time of the 1938 hurricane in which many elms fell, a sadly stalwart army. He is puzzled that they all do not fall in the same direction, to point the same way. But interlace, across the streets, holding hands or limbs. All day the wind roars. They wait outside, to see what the next move will be. We include them. We take them outside. They have died many times before or else have moved away, into other towns, and take off their sad uniforms, one by one, and lay down at last in holes which they have dug in the earth. It is sad, to think of autumn, and the wind blowing, and the elm trees having leaves blown off, and the police and us moving to other towns and taking off our uniforms. We prefer fire. We would that it were firemen we were. We were.

Big firemen. Little firemen. In the flames they are dancing. *Fire delights in its form.* Firemen delight in their form? Inform us, policemen. We call upon them to inform us. Hence all the beatings and the shootings and the putting into closed places behind doors. Firemen and snowmen share other fates, the one burning, the one melting. Snow delights in its form, being mutable. It is the immutable that despairs. At least for a time, for any other time, for all time, for bygone times, for times past, for time enough, for in time. Time will tell.

The clock, on the wall, walks to the door. The door, in the wall, walks to the stair. The stair, up the wall, walks to the window, both ways.

X speaks of which way the road should be one way, whether to go up the hill, which results in the grinding roar of motors and less speed. Or down the hill, which results in the smoothing lag of motors and more speed. Principles of activity are first. Because they are first, they are not second, and so what is second has uniquely the condition of being first, in that respect. Or if what is first is not second, then the first of being second is to be the first second. There are sixty seconds in a minute but no firsts. The first second is that moment when the gun is caused to fire, and whatever activity it signals to begin, does begin. That is the first second. The second second is the one that comes after. In the ritual of *count down,* there is a curious reversal experienced as five, four, three, two, one. Five. Four. Three. Two. One. Note that one is not only not first, or second, but last, which is

immutable, therefore despairs. Being neither first, nor second, nor even fifth, which in other worlds it might be in that hope might there exist, it is the last one. Despair is the absence of hope. X speaks of the despair of the road being presently both ways. There is no way to go on a road that goes always. One way will not be another way.

X speaks of the necessity of deciding, before the police come. We call the firemen and they come. They have uniforms too but they do not all have them or they do not have all of them. The uniforms have whatever firemen they have and so do the firemen. There is instantly, first and second, a relaxation of tensions. They fight fire, for example, but though they burn, they do not fight themselves. We all burn and enjoy the paradox of firemen. Snowmen melt, with the first soft breeze, with the trickle of freshening water, with the budding crocus, with the warmth returning. *Où sont les neiges d'antan?* Oh, watery bodies! X speaks of the road on which snow has never fallen? Oh, trackless wastes, oh, driving snow. You have driven away from us, melting friend, wet hand. Your gentle, fluttering flakes must live in other climes. A hill elsewhere.

This is the despair of being none, or last, or first. Upon that trackless waste, faceless, upon a hill in Darien, Connecticut where the traffic is endless, the cars immutable albeit they rust, both ways. The traffic goes all ways. Call the police, please.

Call the president. He is first, and second to none. His road goes one way and the cars go slowly, thoughtfully, upon it. The snow falls upon it and the snowmen come. The firemen come and the house burns. The wind blows. The elms fall down, pointing one way. Melting away.

Y speaks of other needs, bodily needs, needs of the mind. She wears two hats, of which one is put upon another, but each is first. Her head is small and comfortable. Her hair is long and brown. Her hats are black and brown. Her eyes are brown, her dress is brown, her feet are brown, her house is burning. Call the firemen.

Please. Call the police please.

•

How do you know someone. These typical meetings, and all the people that come of them and to them. The rain on the roof makes a persistent, nostalgic pattering and the music seems a faintly saccharine sadness and he sits with that expected catch in the throat, thinking back and back. He wants to locate a specific place he thinks to remember, and also the company of that afternoon, a then pleasant woman he had known at first almost casually and then with increasingly confused desperation.

It is a somewhat flat place, this area, with unobtrusively present trees in designed patterns. It seems to him that a discretion of paths leads to a common center at which point occurs a statue of some sort, of a person, modestly contained. It is not, as he recalls, a soldier or figure of that sort. Rather, it seems to him a man who is standing, but possibly sitting, with hands rather close to the body, although extended. But there is no assertion, either of offering or of taking, in the gesture.

They have chosen a bench adjacent to the statue and now look out upon the diversity of the regular paths coming to this one center. There seem to be hedges, in his memory, but again they make no abrupt intrusion upon the view. They are of such height and substance that they permit sight of those approaching, or retreating, from approximately the waist, or in some cases the chest, of persons thus passing to and fro. Children are seen as specific heads and at times raised arms or active gestures of one sort and another. It is all very quiet in tone. The sky is typically English, as one says, a severely grey overcast although rain falls only as a drizzle, and this occurs but rarely.

It is comfortable, to be sitting here. The rain seems forgotten, the music fades. Their comfort is secure as they sit, and they have eaten but shortly before and done the divers things they had thought to, a phone call or two as also the mailing of his several letters.

There are also birds, distinctly. He cannot remember of what kind, precisely, since they also take place in this grey condition and have neither size nor plumage that would make them appear decisive. Possibly they are pigeons of the common variety, grey checks or bars with occasional splashes of dull white. If there is an occasional red, it is so flattened by both bird's condition and the greyness that it becomes as if one with the others. Or they are sparrows, unobtrusively fluttering and pecking, almost noiseless.

There is much to talk about, it seems, but for the moment they are content to sit. Quite probably he has taken her hand, or she his, and they lean back together against the bench's support. The hour argues no necessities, and for this moment the complexities of what either considers their lives are in abeyance. Think, then, of a muted calm much like the edges of lakes at twilight.

Looking, he sees, marked by the hedges, the line of the people coming and going. For a moment, one in particular appears as a head only, but it is not a child's. It has a decided mustache, carefully clipped, and wears on its head a homburg. He looks as intently as he dares but realizes that the man is becoming aware of his staring, so turns quickly to look elsewhere. In the new direction he sees nothing untoward for some time. Children, with their nurse, whom they are exhorting in clear, high voices to accompany them

to the statue, are the only immediate presences. Reassured, he follows them with his eyes, so that he finds himself with them, as a group, centered upon the statue. But this also, he recognizes, has changed. As the children come up to it, the youngest, a boy, climbs up on its slight pedestal, then stands upright, holding on to the statue's back. Remarkably he seems to tower above it, and waves to the nurse, and the two small girls who must be his sisters, to see him in his new vantage. The nurse calls the boy down, impatiently, seemingly irritated that the public monument might be injured in some way.

Here the rain has now stopped and moments ago the kitten was playing on the bed, then moved about the small room until it mewed to be let out again. The music has changed to, "Back in the Saddle Again . . ." Gabby Hayes. He is discomforted by both sides of the reality, the mirror. He had not remembered the place so vividly as he now seemed to. There are patches of wet steam on the lower panes of the windows. The flame of the small pipelike stove burns blue. The light beside his right hand makes an intensive center of illumination upon the paper. Something like that. He lights a cigarette again.

It was in memory that this scale of things shifting was particularly interesting to him. He knew of those constructed rooms used for purposes of psychiatric analysis in which perspectives may be altered to accommodate the patient's experience of the spatial relationships of substances on an apparently fixed plane of reference. But he could not remember, now, whether it was the father whose chair grew large, in perspective, or was it the father himself? The room tilted. That door, so looming, was actually the measure of a small box. He could see everything. There were no dark-nesses despite the greyness of the weather. But the scale was insistently changing. She continued to have his hand in her own and both sat without speaking, in a pleasant quiet. He was curious to know whether or not she had been also wit-ness to what now so displaced him despite its lack of threat. The boy, certainly, was none, was, in fact, charming, with his red cheeks and alert movement. Although he could not see them as clearly, hidden, in a sense, as both now were back of the statue, with only the nurse's torso fully apparent, the girls too he found cheering.

He reviewed his initial sense of the place. Its absence in time gave it curiously vague location finally but by a process of pacing, in his mind, he felt himself to have placed it with some accuracy. If one moved that way, then the street was along the path a short walk's distance. If left, then again a street appeared in a relatively brief time. The park itself he saw as basically a square whose diagonals were the paths, or the major ones because he thought there were possibly two others whose direction ran parallel to the outline of the park itself, composing two smaller squares, in that way, within it. He was sure that hedges outlined all the paths and that there were also trees at various intervals, in fixed pattern, and that flowers grew, in discreet beds, at various points but these he could not give decisive place to. In like confusion he could not distinctly remember the color of his friend's dress, or coat, or whether she sat to his left or to his right. He was reluctant to disturb their own quiet and so said nothing to her.

People continued passing up and down the various walks. He found that he could continue to watch them without

their awareness of it by fixing his eyes on some object slightly beyond their actual location. A woman with an extraordinarily elongated chest but with head markedly smaller came past, her lower half cut off by the hedge. Two large heads followed her. A dog, barking, jumped suddenly above the hedge, like a whale sounding. The statue itself seemed to dwindle increasingly. Perhaps it was the lengthening of the afternoon that created the impression. He looked at his watch and saw that they would soon have to move in order to keep an appointment for tea. Yet he could not shift his attention from what he was seeing it was so calmly fascinating.

He recalls now many things, many people. He thinks of a beach in Truro, in Deya, in Gloucester, in San Diego. He puts people on it, many men and many women, and many children. Dogs run past. Divers things are dropped, lost in the sand. The water comes up on the beach, goes back on the beach, with the tides. Why should *size* be so insistent a center. Is it simply that a toy car won't hurt you and a real one will? He couldn't accept the isolation of condition implicit in that logic. The big man wants to help you, the little one hasn't the strength?

But their heads and *that* insistent variation was a matter of different kind. He felt the pressure of her hand tighten and, looking at her, felt it then simple to call her attention to the phenomenon with which he had been, for so long, preoccupied. But how could he reach her, then. Way off she was somewhere, truly somewhere else. He could take an actual map and with a pin make precise her location, but here she was not. He crawled into the core of the telephone wires and pushed with all his strength to make a way. Foolish. He wrapped himself with paper, scrunched down into the ink, licked, then patted, and sealed it all over him, then stamped it. All the same, impossible. He was always too big, too small, it didn't really matter.

The people go on walking. It is really a matter of indifference who comes and goes there, assuming they treat one another with courtesy.

•

2·3·1

Two

Look, look. The road home. Some one. The road knows. The rose nose. He sees what he says. And says what he sees. There. Here. It isn't very big. But then. It isn't very small. It. Is in the middle.

Come in. At last the door opens and into the warmth of the small but humanly cosy room step two onions. Neither knows what road they have taken, or been taken, or even will take. They will not talk about it. Their faces betray a green and ruddy reverence. Their reference is belief. True believers two, too. They come in also. Chairs are offered all four, but sans legs or even arms wherewith to balance upon the center of such possibility they choose to roll down on the floor, all four thus on all fours. A heap.

The fire burns low. No other light or lights lighten the living room, which it is. Discover that wood speaks. Never to be forgotten the first saw it saw. It hurts, ripping the tender interlocking tissues, rasping, ripping, scraping, unfeeling such saws. Agh. Onions were better although knives come too, often in pairs. Is it the fire that wants wood. Or paper. The house will not burn simply to be obliging. Sometimes it will. But only once. Think of that. Ones. They come in pairs. The road follows its nose. The house will not burn. The fire burns low. Wood speaks. Chairs are awful. On all fours, onions.

It becomes time to cook. They have always liked cooking, the empty pots and pans, the torn paper, little bits of this and that. Too many cooks, or two mommy cooks. They will. And it is ready. Eat. But wait for mommy, or many, as they come. It is too low for the window, but gets a chair, careful to step on no onion, or fire. Sees out. There, there, there. She is coming. Down the road. How good the hills of home, or wherever they are met with. Up and down, a delightful pastime. They are sure. Dancing is for girls. And boys. Boys and girls and onions make a delightful repast. Just in time.

Mommy is here. First her feet, first her hair, first her before, first her behind. The door knows the doorknob. Opens and in the openness of the opening, mommy comes in, all over. Mommy comes all over everything. With everything. Just in time insofar as it is a place to be. So happy to have her come. Eat.

Without the road noone knows. Without the door. Without the window. Without the wind blowing. Without the sky is blue. Without the moon shines on. Without the rain and April flowers. Where have we been, then. So long. So far. So big. So little. So much. So what. Always comes true, two of them. Bringing home the onions. Bringing home the bacon. Unfriendly persons. Diga me, las personas vayan. Right on, old buddy. You speak good. In two tongues. In two heads, too. Two is the number for you.

Stretching out, having eaten. Everything. All done. No more. It's all gone now. Poor wood. Poor house. Think. Doors on everything, all locked. Her arms full of packages, she fumbles for the key. The door opens and looks out. She, full of packages, looks in. In and out. Up and down. Same thing. She knows she is home. Home free, they say, the whole house shouting. Come in. Pleasure is such a delight. Yes, yes. How good. How bad to be good. How good to be bad. Up and down. In and out. Here. There. The window. Moves the chair over, awful, to see there. Two. Mommy. Full of onions, who have things they can too do. By mommy. Sit down. You

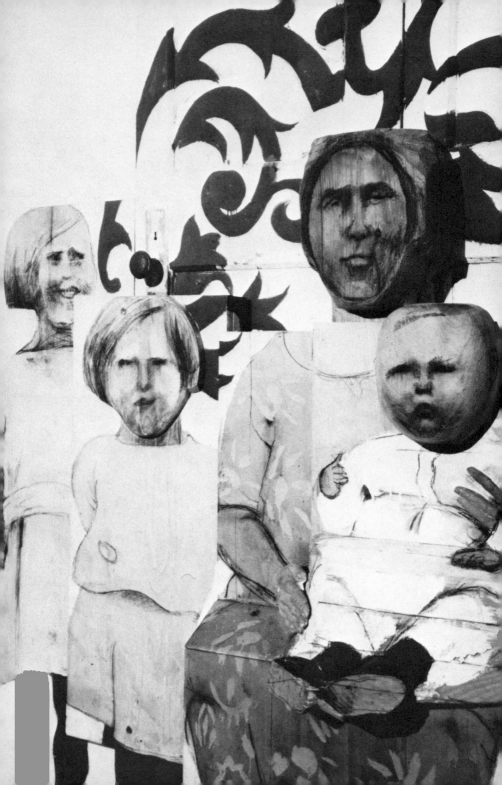

have been long gone, you have come. Home. The hills. The valleys. The sun. The moon. The ups. The downs. The moors. The arabs. Singing light flies forth through valley floor to topmost tip of tree stands up to see the singing light. Lights and livers, clouds and onions. Eat. You are home. You may rest assured. This is what home has come to know and be known as home. Forever.

But outside you can look in, or inside you can look out, or up, down, or down, up. Think. Who is mommy, who is she, that all those saints have fainted. The sky, guy, the lid, kid. Can you ride a rocking horse, billy boy, billy boy. Singing light. The sun has come and made the moon to shine again on all, on all fours on the floor. Takes a load off its feet. A load in his pants. Her hand in his. Just under the skin. They dance with ants in their pants. New arrivals. Telegrams. Boats pulled up on the shore for the night. Low voices. Muttering fires. Silent stars. The universe is one. Universe.

A place in the sun, a place in the dark, how good to be home, when it comes time to sit down, just in time, her arms full of packages, a load in his pants. The couple are truly two and too true. The sun is shining. Singing light. At night he walks out under the stars, and looks up. At night he wakes up under the stairs and lets down. A huge load. A big one. But bigger two. Two heads are better than one, requiring no hat. Where did you leave it. Out there. Incredible, ecstatic distances discovered narrowly missing. Take your onions with you. When you go out to play. Stay. Out of the road. A voice singing light. And low. And know to go home before asked to. Good manners. Good night. Good day to you, dos personas. You have come far, to come here. Come in. Home. Come in, billy. Over and out. By which action leans heavily on her head, causing her pain.

The first night. Home. The second night, home, the third, home, the fourth, night. Home game. Plays in the park. A ball.

Always does what told to. Always. Mommy. Remembers mommy as onions, full of packages. Buys boys. Just in time. This time. That time. A time too.

Quicker, slower. The hills seem to lengthen in the last light. Stretching. So far to get to know. Home. No one home. Always two. One wants two. Dig it. Me too, las personas. So charming they have come. Home. Home to mommy more than one to keep the home fires burning. Saw a saw. The wood works. Without the rain but safe inside, again. They have always liked cooking, little bits of this and that. Mommy comes too. But only once. A heap. Right on. In two tongues. In two heads. Is the number for you too.

Mommy. Come home.

•

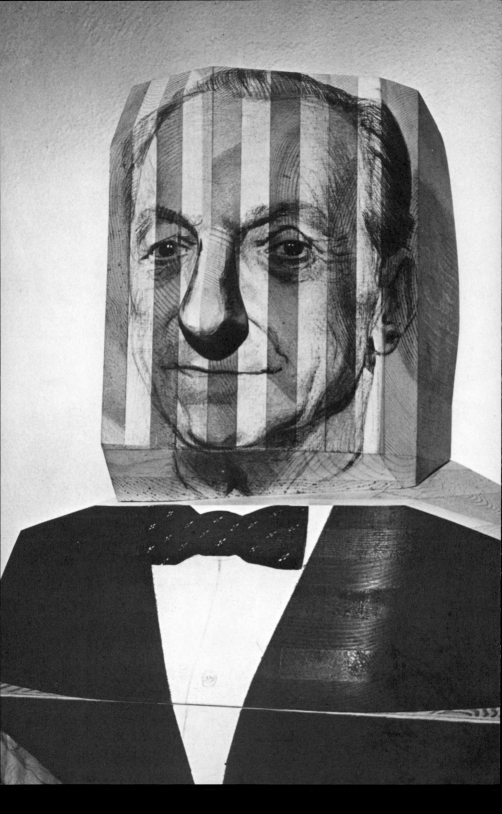

One morning you wake up in bed five feet tall, or six, or eight feet tall. Something has happened. You lie and look at your feet, way down there. Your hands extend on the ends of two elongated arms and if you move them in arcs, they seem the measure of the spheres. Neither securing nor disquieting, this change. More probably it has happened to you because you have come upon it, fallen upon it, as it were, and stretching, it's all very true.

You were out all night, possibly, and perhaps the night, even nights, before. You were walking but in the dark and given the faint path you were trying to follow, you had fallen several times. At one time you went down several feet, into a somewhat steep though small ravine, and lay at the bottom, looking up to see the dense dark forms of trees against a faintly lighter blue-black sky. Fog lay deeper than yourself, in soft pockets down the lower traces of the ravine. No sounds, really. Now and then some snatch of talking, some creak of wood, a falling star possibly, sounding a streak of peripheral tears.

You wanted to cry, you were so happy. Sad? Could not altogether remember. The one thing changes the other. No two at the same time, somehow, despite it insistently happens. What you were was young. Old? More probably older, as it's said of those who have come to be here. There. "He finally got here." But he was going there.

You watch him as backward, into, a mirror you, in looking, are. He does not see you, he is you. Or her, or them. They are several ones all in one. You love him because you love yourself, loving him, yourself.

You move, looking for places where you may meet. She must be somewhere else now. No wish to take her life into yours in just this way. Falling down is hard to do. Certainly as an accompaniment to someone else's. Though they fall into each other's arms every time.

This warm specificness of bodies, you think. Eight feet tall, eight inches, six or five. The trees look across at you, equal height. A level regard as on a plain or bus station, eyes meet. You meet her walking and look into her eyes, so lovely, lovely wit to them, seeing you. You climb over her body. You remember mountains in New Hampshire. You think of things to do. Rainy days in Massachusetts, a barn with hay mows. You wriggle into the hay, burrowing down, and come, head first, to the metal basket for the horse's hay, placed at the edge of the ceiling and wall. You look out, upside down, taking deep breaths since you have just arrived at the surface, into the horse's deeply soft dark eyes. It loves you. It is not your horse. The barn creaks with sounds of timber shifting, loose boards, and on the main floor with its heavy planking, your feet resonate with heavy sure footsteps.

Today you are a man. Yesterday you were a man. A week ago you were a man but no one had told you. A letter, indescribable, had been mailed years before. There was need to establish your own identity before it could be given you insofar as it was specific, although you didn't know it. It was waiting.

You were waiting, all your life. It was not a long time. You woke up, in bed, elongated. Your mother was far away. Your father, dead. These specific relationships, all wrong. Unmeaning more than being there, too, you thought. The sun

burned through the window and seized your face warmly.

You wanted to be in France, Spain, but you were not. You insisted on home as a place you know, and forgot it. People you loved, had loved, cried out in pain, unwitting, inconstant, helpless. You saw children in large crowds coming toward you, arms up in the air, calling out to you to acknowledge them, to come to them, with them. You wanted to, you thought, but your size as you stood out and up from the bed brushed the ceiling. You were irrevocably in the room.

You would never leave it. You had come to it, into it, and gone to sleep, her long warm hair over your face. Breathing deeply. Unthinking, slept there, with her. You woke up and explored her, climbed all over her, took with your hand, her hand, and touched her. Deeply. Soft, wet, warmly, and talks to you of yourself, all alone.

A voice in your ear shouts, *mangia!* An agreement to eat as the huge boat flounders on through waves of water. You have consented, through need, to be put in its very bottom, and sleep on one of a rack of beds, which reach up to the ceiling. You wake up and see a face, eagerly intent, very close to your own, shouting. He cares for you as an old world person cares for his brothers. He is sweet and thoughtful, but very loud. It is time to eat. It is not time to eat. An hour goes by. You walk through the maze of stairs and gangways to the dining room and join your friends, a man and woman, sitting at a small table, waiting, smiling as you sit down too. She has lovely deep breasts, long waist, full body. He is intelligently wry, open to amusement, and blond. They like to dance.

You step out, you jump, back, forward. You find yourself confused in the literal place. You reach around yourself, feel bodies, women. You know them but are restless, and twist away. Someone on the stairs, going up, takes your hand and looks at it, smiling. She admires its strength and width of palm. He tells you you have painters' hands. You smile with pleasure, you never forget either of them, but they do not really know each other, nor ever did, or will. It is several places you live in, the horse's nuzzling as you pull clear of the hay and drop into its stall, the woman, the women's nuzzling, the man's smile.

You step over them, you drop back into the bed, alone now. The sun rises steadily, into the sky. You go with it, fall back, get up, lie down, walk slowly forward, then run. You can make out the forms of the trees, in the fog, darkness. No moon this night to help you. You remember your way, feeling forward with your feet the nature of the path you are trying to follow. You have come back to leave again. You want no one to see you come or go.

You are very big, you think. You were small, a speck merely, a twinkle in the universe. You have come here to continue and will never stop again. You think it all goes on forever and will go insistently with it. Here, there, you run back and forth. You are in love again.

You love it that you are in love again. You are eight feet tall, waking up. You are alone. You are crying, you are smiling with simple pleasures, you know everything, you know nothing.

You want to get home now. The boat plunges on. You walk

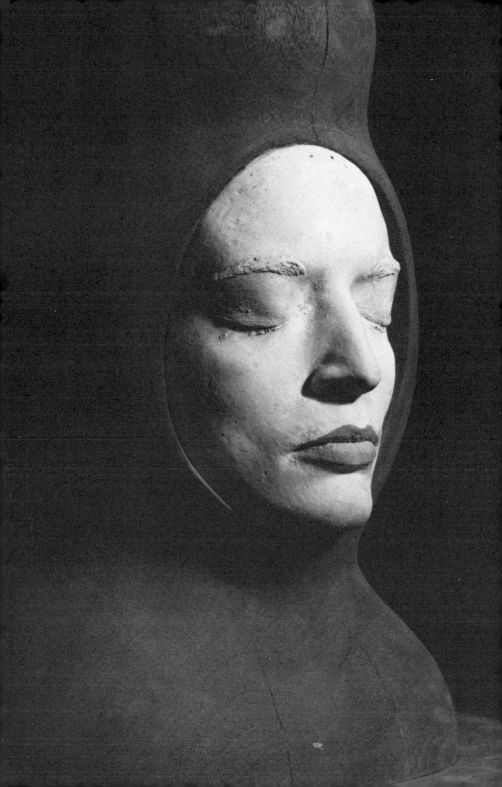

to the bow with your two friends. She places herself at the very point of ship's forward timbers. The wind blows strongly. The man watches, smiling, and from time to time asks questions about life in Spain. She does a little dance, long hair swinging, and you mime it with gestures of your strong hands.

The woman is back of you, behind you at a great distance, driving a small sports car whose owner had been her sister's husband. She is going somewhere but thoughts do not show it clearly. You look around intently and recognize nothing. It is fall, or spring, with the leaves coming out, or dropping off, the trees. You feel the changes insistently. You want to go back, or forward, to where it all was, is, will be.

You have suddenly changed your name again. It is unpronounceable. Something like Harry, or Bill, or Jim perhaps. You cannot remember. It seems to go with the great size of your body. The boat is nearing land, you think. You try to get the small number of your possessions together and put within simple reach. You go again to the bow of the boat and look out, thinking to see something. The effect is of much water, sky, and a few circling birds you note are gulls. There will be a last party tonight, on ship board, a farewell. You know that your friends will not leave you since they are going to the same place. You sit at table with them and drink all of the red wine that the ship provides. Later you go with them to the bar, then dance with them.

You are thinking of explanations. It is as if it never happened so you cannot believe there is reason to be more concerned than that. Then you are crying, uncontrollably, and you are, insistently, asking all who will stop for your questions, what it has all been about. You rehearse your own explanations over and over but they are incomplete. You wait for it to end. You see the end coming, you think.

You have been away. The boat approaches the dock assigned to it and modestly the trip is over. You see your friends already taking place in the line of people who will shortly be leaving. You want to wave to them but realize you are leaving too.

Perhaps it is too late. At last you get into the line and are slowly taken off the boat as it moves forward. You look shyly out of your eyes to see who is waiting. You see her at some distance, at the edge of the crowd. She is very small, perhaps shrunken. You ease your bulk forward, waving to her, and her eyes meet the middle of your chest. You lift her in your arms with your hands to kiss her. You both go home.

•

The day grows misty with incoming fog. Just out the window a large, leaning tree-stump and an oil barrel, upended, gone green in lovely manner. A slow day, waiting for rain. Flowers lift to go stiff at the edges of their leaves, curling. Things grow, crashing up, and tops then die, and the lower parts of the plant go brown and die too. Everything expanding, as far as it can.

There are monsters in the desert, who prey on the unwary. Tales record as much as such ever leaves behind. Windy bones bleaching, like they say. This time they got wise, they thought, and made extensive preparations so as not to let these monsters have their way with them, however many there were in fact in the company. Forty, say. More like two hundred. At least a very distinct number of these people. What they do is get lots of water in big casks and water bags and all that sort of container and they load the mules and the camels, all that they have to hoist this stuff forward into the desert of their desire. They have the monsters completely buffaloed, so they figure, because they are not going to run out of water out there and drop down on their knees in the sand with their tongues going black and their eyes popping out, etc.

So off they go, a great day, bands playing, mothers waving, wives, daughters, the otherwise left at home. This is really going to be it. The monsters know they are coming just that that is what monsters are there to know, but they just let it keep happening as these others think it really is. First night comes and the enthusiasts really think they've got it made as they guzzle their plenteous water. They are even splashing it around a little until the one who has got the whole idea in his head, the leader, says to quiet down and get some sleep and don't waste the water needlessly. He says that not harshly because he knows there is so much water on those mules and camels they could almost float to that other place they are going to. Next day dawns bright and early, and they plunge on. Things are creaking a bit, water is heavy, but they keep moving in the same good spirits, rolling along. Comes the third day, the fourth day, things are basically the same, but the fifth day it is really getting a little heavy. Like, who needs all that water.

So the commander gets them all around the campfire that night and gives it to them straight. Men, desert is dry and this one has monsters, and that water is all we've got. Right. So up again the next morning, and onward. But this is not a morning like any other because now they see coming toward them another huge caravan in a factually weird condition. All the people are wet, really soaking, and they are slogging along as if it was raining cats and dogs. All the wagons are slugging through mud and the people's hair is plastered down and it really is totally wet. They see one guy with his mouth full of watercress, then another. Wow.

Naturally they ask what's up. Oh, say these wet people, you see that green line way over there. Past that line, it's raining all the time and that's where we've come from and you're going. So that's what, say the first guys, and instantly smash all their casks of water and their barrels. Forget it. Then they go on, find no water, drop down in desert, and the monsters eat them.

•

3·1·2
Three

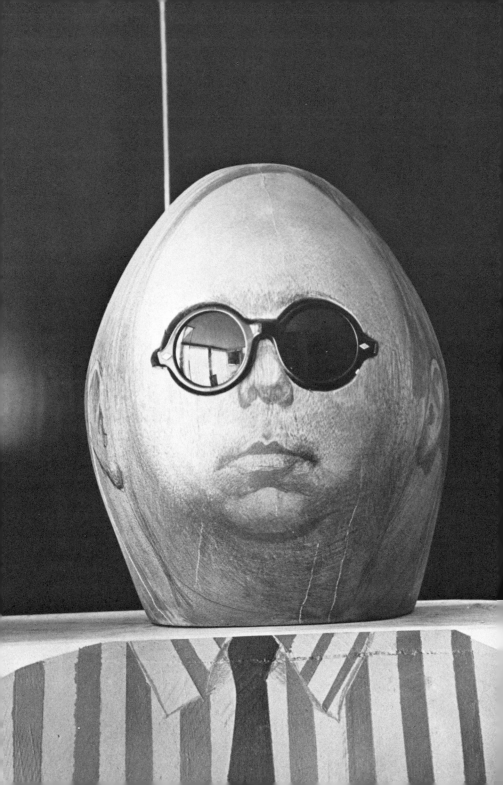

In those days we were trying to play football in the lot back of the school close to the pine trees. Mr. Scribner was our coach, volunteer, and also Harry's father. His clothing is hard to remember except that every Memorial Day he put on his old army uniform and marched with the VFW section of the parade down the main street of the town and finally to the cemetery not far from where we were then living. On the days we played football he often wore an old-style football helmet, with distinct pieces it seemed, so that the ear flaps especially hung down like sewed on patches. He, Harry, and the others, Marilyn, Stevie, younger children and Mrs. Scribner, all lived in an apartment in a house owned by Miss Boston, a curious English woman who often went riding on an old horse in complete riding habit. The Scribner family were her especial responsibility and so she provided both dwelling and odd jobs for Mr. Scribner, who did no other work we knew of.

So he was free to teach us, as now football, and that we learned in the classic form of the early 1900s. To block the opposing team, our line, on the snap of the ball back, turned to face sideways the person next to us, not our opponents but our teammates, whereupon we fell down and rolled over. This proposed an instant jumble and thus a confusion of bodies through which the other team's players would not be able to pass. We practiced this maneuver persistently and it is the one thing clearly remembered from all those afternoons, late sun and tumbling and lots of shouting and the trees that kept still and watched.

Otherwise, marching along those streets in the parade, uniform always feeling incomplete, perhaps the kerchief wrong, or the shoes not the kind stipulated by assumed regulations, or the body just not fitting it, even the feet trying to catch up, Mr. Scribner was so quietly and generously reassuring to ourselves. We wanted it. We would do anything to be with it. One Halloween night we were trying to think of some immense displacement of the town's usual conduct but only the big boys could really make it. They took the billboards with the political campaign images and hoisted them on to roofs, and even got an old car up on top of Mr. Grey's house. But they were too fast for us. We'd get there but whatever we had had in mind would be gone. So this night we were soaping, slowly, the window of the town's one dry goods store and were so absorbed by that activity, that we didn't see or hear Pat Foley, the town policeman, coming up behind us in the dark. So there he was and because he couldn't grab all of us, he grabbed one, saying, I've got you, Fred Bird. Boys, come back. Somehow, with an instant agreement, we jumped him, amazed, and held on, whereupon he let go of Fred and we all ran off, scared and heroic, into the dark.

Then one day Ralph and me, Luxie we used to call him, had wandered off from school down to Mac MacGregor's, who owned the town's garage and kept homers, racing pigeons, in a big attic over the garage itself. That was where Rat used to work, a bullet headed, muscled young man with slicked back blond hair and scarey insistent eyes. His information attracted us, as did Mac's, but Mac, being older, got bored with our interest. Rat, on the other hand, would hint endlessly of thefts and deals, and of women seduced, fucked, buggered, raped, torn, eaten. We always stood a little way back from him but we listened to every word he said. His obscenities particularly now come back, the hissing almost spit tone of his words. Later we heard he was taken off to prison.

This afternoon we were just walking toward the garage and were involved with a sort of chant concerning the school's principal. It was a lazy late spring day and we kicked stones or occasional bottles as we went, keeping the unison of *Huff, Huff, the great big puff!* We came into the garage still chanting and to our so-called consternation, suddenly woke to Mr. Huff's actuality, literally before us. His car, a Model A, sat with hood up just beyond him. He looked at us very harshly, asked us what we thought we were doing, and gave instructions that we should see him in his office the next morning. That subsequent encounter now fades though the memory of the way the boards of the school room floor were oiled, and how they smelled, and of wet coats and boots hung in the hall, and light through windows into large rooms, and the varnish—even of faces, of the girl's who had epilepsy, who sat in the desk in front of me so that her head, during a seizure, would fall back on my desk top—all that stays put.

She was a shy girl and the seizures really embarrassed her. I felt for her very much since I had a glass eye that would with my rubbing at it as the school day got tedious occasionally fall out and roll across the floor under the desks. Always some pleasantly intrigued and brave kid would pick it up, ask permission to leave his seat, and bring it back to me. I would rub it with my handkerchief, an instance of which I still compulsively keep with me, though the eye itself is long gone, and put it back in. At recess kids I wasn't friends with would tease me by asking, did I take it out with a spoon, and then plead to see it. Was it round and so forth. One so maddened me I remember jumping him and finally pounding his head against the metal supports for the swings until friends of us both pulled me off.

I couldn't keep my temper easily. My mother used to say, count ten. My friends had an endless variation of ritual for not letting them get at you. I would be fine for awhile but then it would just blow up in my head, and I'd jump. Often it was sadly actual friends I attacked, like Buddy Butler, with whom I fought when we were both in the seventh grade, out in the school grounds, surrounded by those specious, provoking onlookers, until we were both so exhausted we could neither of us hold on to anything nor lift our arms anymore. One other kid, a bully, really wore down on me until one day, as I was going through the hall to get the bus, he flashed past slapping my books out of my arms to the floor. Happily I nailed him, with a quick punch on the nose, which bled, transforming him to a weeping, sad kid.

Myself is what one comes to think of, then, letting the well fill up, things happen. Others out there, like June Welsh, who was a welfare kid living on the DeSouza farm up from where we did. Beauteous June, round faced, short bob, so tough and so tender. She caught at one's heart with her human vulnerability and to walk home with her was to enter such deep pride and confusion. Or Helen, seemingly tall, Scandinavian, her brother for a time my sister's boyfriend so that she and I were likewise linked. Tilda, whose brother was my own friend and whose father thought I should devote myself to latin, and the outwitting of the Catholic conspiracy. Days and nights no doubt forever.

Persons and things moving in and out of that place make a part of it. The Batemans came late, moving into a house down the street from us, two boys, mother and father, which last opened a small store in the main part of the town. Both

parents were faint sort of people, that is, ok but we sure didn't figure they were like Mr. Scribner or Mac or Mrs. Locke, who made the traditionally world's greatest chocolate cake. These people tended to keep to themselves, nice but really not there. The kids thus had no real center either to come from or to bring us to. The older was our age and came into what we were doing as we needed someone to play right field or to keep a look out or to ask some awkward question of people we'd prefer not to talk to. So he got along.

But the younger was really alone, there being no kids of his own age close enough to get to nor our own real permission, and particularly not his brother's who was told by his parents to take care of him, hence wanted him gone. This kid was spunky. You could knock him down time after time, tease him endlessly, but when the dust cleared, there he was, coming back. He even got a kind of mad clarity out of it and that tinge of really heroic singleness which can be entirely present, no matter the circumstance. He believed everything we said so that was our advantage. For example, we played our version of cowboys and indians in the woods back of my house. It was really settlers and indians and so we had the clearing, which was where the settlers were established and then all the woods around it, thick with impending indians. Word would come that the indians were massing for an attack on our humble defenses. So we'd hold a conference, to which this kid was also invited, and come to common decision that our best defense was offense, and so all of us set out to attack the indians with the one exception of the kid whom we told had to be there, to keep the camp together. Once out of his sight we were instant indians and howled horrible execrations at the white man for his encroachments on the red man's lands. These consisted mainly of threats to cut off the heads of, the testicles of, the hands and feet of any white dog met with. From time to time one of us would dash through the clearing where the kid sat by this time bawling with terror, to scream, they're right behind me, then disappear.

Only literal fatigue ever ended that one, and it always worked. The sobbing kid would be reassured it was all a game, then he would slowly stop crying, pleased we were all back, and then, very possibly, it would all begin again. We just couldn't believe it was so simple.

But one time I remember it went, in that classic way, beyond expectation. It was an afternoon and both of his parents were gone, his brother too, and him, and me, and possibly one other kid were out in a small pasture, partly an apple orchard, close to his house. It was fall and the apples apparently were of no interest to the farmer who owned the pasture. We found a few we could eat but most were on the ground, rotten. So we were fooling around with the rotten apples, throwing them at rocks, the trees, occasionally at each other, until we hit on the plan of daring the kid to throw them at his own house, which was white clapboards. We helped him by hauling large quantities to a place where he'd have an easy chance of hitting it, and so he began. Big brown splotches began to appear as the kid lobbed one after another, delighted with his own ability. Finally we wanted him to stop, fearing he'd spill our whole involvement to his parents, but he was far beyond us and the last memory is him still throwing, it's almost dark now, and the car drives into the yard.

•

"And there's some milk." "It's very interesting." "That's out of sight."

It's a funny experience, you see? To go see something like that. A lot of the time I'm in, I think. Like a hole, to keep in one place. You're thinking. Tom leaving, and going over to visit Magda. Not heavily, he's got a beautiful, wise, intuitive sense of where it is. If I started doing the thing with my head, it would be very hard to keep doing this.

"A rhythmic experience." "The steady thing."

Making that be your secret guide but not your outspoken guide. Oh, I think so. Beautiful, wise, intuitive sense of where it is. Turned on. Waist deep, amidst the encircling gloom. The intimacy of the sounds in the house were first, like they say, a kind of displacement. Yah. Music interferes, spheres.

"You get here are mostly all your own sounds."

To get it on, but it sounds like. The kind of music that was happening around here when everybody just sits in and tries to make music together. Peter turned me on to African music. To create it if you were particularly serious. I didn't find that experience anything like what I'd think it would be at all.

"Particularly serious and disciplined." "Just because I realized the kind of music that was happening around here."

Harmony is just like what your ear says like. Your own sounds except for cars. I love the sounds though. Open, marshmallow? That's the same thing with clapping. Ah, ecstatic. Open note to the possibility of something happening. Open. Swamp mellow. What are you saying, you like this house? It's entirely intimate.

"Like they say, a kind of displacement." "Tum, tum." "What do you mean by being turned on?"

Know any keep doing this. Making that be your secret guide but not your outspoken guide. There's some milk. Then I've already thought of it. Like I got into a hole. A whole imaginary trip. It stays steady. Making that be your secret guide but not your outspoken guide. Intuitive sense of where it is. It's absolutely everything.

"Then it's impeccable." "Ah, ecstatic."

Cut it out! I really like this though. Way down upon. There's such a metronomic. Tum, tum. Like resonates all through. Weird discomfort. You do? Just basic beats. Like I'd been listening to African music, you know. Made music seem like what you could only manage to listen to. I was playing second violin. It's the same experience when it starts happening.

"They really mean it. Coming back, I realized I played in music. Only what you could manage to create if you were particularly serious and disciplined. The beats, and then the variation on the beats. Yah. Tum, tum. Open up anything. How do you get yourself turned on then. Beautiful, wise, intuitive sense of where it is. But not your outspoken guide. A whole imaginary trip."

•

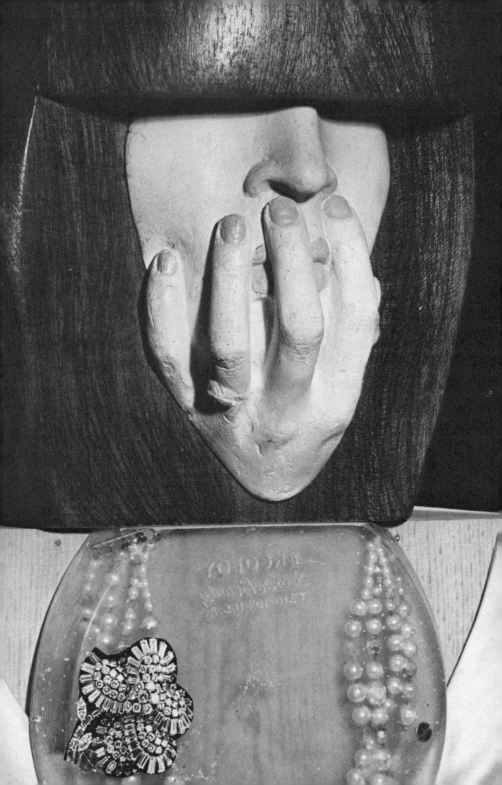

Voices fading fast. He turns in a circle to find them again. Sense from movies of fun house mirrors and, *this way, Harry, I'm over here.* Bang. Another mirror bites the dust. He throws his now useless gun at the multiple images and turns, to think.

Perchance to dream, like they say. Think it over and come back on Monday. No one ever quite wrong enough. So far. No one ever quiet enough. To hear them.

Meeting Mabel again after forty years, he was struck by the fact she was still alive. In fact, pretty. Pretty good enough is enough for me, he was thinking. He turned to smile. She was thinking of the time they had first met, on a dock in downtown Boston. Waiting for a bust.

Not funny, McGee. Simple laughter from the outside looking in. Pains of growing up. Growing pains of larger sizes. Places inside wanting outside. Things to do while waiting to do something.

Why *do* things, she was saying. He stopped as if at a real intersection. I do what comes to hand, he said. Painful, inept moralist, she was thinking, let him eat cake.

Mabel grew incontinently while waiting for time to pass, in the several places she found herself in, waiting. The voices fade fast, in fact, the first to go, leaving the rest to follow if they can. She was a girl, then woman, then a fading voice of herself in inept moral circumstance, waiting. She loves everything, he thought. He remembered the first time in Boston as if the dream were really true. Is this him, he said to Mabel, as they sat in a room, looking at one another. The man on the can is the owner perhaps. See baby food image of man now big, with life changed by hitting wall in race car at excessive speed. Nothing changes he hadn't thought of. Instant real. Truth's inexorable circumstance. Later.

They were driving under a long succession of viaducts, or overpasses, in a slight rain. The other man's wife was extraordinarily attractive, and she was driving them home. The other man drove the other car. At some point not simply to be determined the lines of movement were no longer congruent and they became divergent, flooded with memories. She could not smile simply as if nothing had happened. She was dreaming a dream of alternatives. She nuzzled the bottle like a horse and laughed at her previous fears. You have nothing to fear but fear itself, looking in the store window, wanting shoes. Congruence of clothing had made them appear the same. An army of marching men. And women. Raincoats and rain hats and galoshes protect them from the heavy downpour. The car passes, spraying sheets of water. They were in love and took no notice of the shouting people. He reached over to take her hand and it came off in his. Her head rolled on the floor. Her eyes dribbled forth. Her ears shattered, face breaking like a tired child's. He took out a gun and shot what was left, disgusted. Then he walked away.

Mabel dusted the furniture again and checked provisions for the drinks. Ice, water, glasses. All was in readiness. She went to the mirror and fell in. Guests arriving a half hour later found the house apparently as ever but water had flooded the basement and was rising rapidly. Also numerous icebergs bumped up under the livingroom floor, nine tenths of them under water, as they knew from childhood. Silly boy, she

said, and ripped his clothes from him with one hand tied behind her back.

They regretted they had not known one another better when the first opportunity had offered. In retrospect they were perfect for one another but now he lived in Africa and she had lost his address. He was also dead, she thought, surely, after all that had happened. He, however, still loved her too, and was sitting beside her on the couch. Mabel, he said, and ripped her clothes from her without even thinking. He lit a cigarette and walked away without a backward glance.

Backward people more retentive of what's present, he thought, waiting for the first signs of life. When the truck hit him, he was really not there. Mabel, unknowing, still waited for the sound of his footsteps, coming up the walk. She had put on her best dress and after seeing to the drinks, she sat on the couch with both hands in her lap. After all these years she knew it was about to happen.

She was in love with another man's life, and wanted to, *go crazy*. When the car hit the wall, he broke everything in his body including the bottle of gin he was bringing to her. It was to have been a happy reunion but it would be some time now, if ever, before it could be thought of. Thoughtful of his condition, the ambulance dropped him off at her corner, waving goodbye.

Mabel knows enough to know better. She listens with both ears. Her head is a radio. Rialto rose, love is the bed she lies in, heat what she turns on. Or up. Smiles through broken teeth. Old rumpled mattress. She felt his hands on her body although he lived in Africa, she remembered. It was a dream in which many things have happened all at once.

Sodden, dreary expectations. He had no impulse even to ring the bell, much less to go into a room he could only feel revolting. How dare she interrupt his life with inept solicitations. He threw the roses to the ground and stamped on them, then left, to his own devices.

Voices fade fast. In the desert the sound extends in asymmetric manner, over hill and hollow, until exhausted, fades out. The last rose of summer, the same. He listens with a marked intentness, turning the volume higher and higher. At last there is a faint, scratching sound. It is from the attic, over his head, where she sleeps alone, head buried in pillow, her eyes a smear of tears.

As soon as you're born, they make you feel small. They are bigger, she says, sneering. He lurches against the fireplace and falls in. She turns off the radio and leaves the room. She says, that's the last time. He is soundless, in the fire. He is thinking of old times, when they tucked him softly into bed, with a good night kiss.

Mabel is the big time but he's blown it, years ago, on the dock in Boston. A grape for your thoughts. Pettiness floods his mind. He rips her clothes from his body with one mind. I do what comes to hand, he said.

●

$$\frac{1 \cdot 2 \cdot 3}{\text{Four}}$$

It is a scene with some distance so that a lake, or sky, floats in the far perspective. Immediately to the left, at the front, is a woman with upper torso clothed in a light hazy autumn brown colored tunic with lower half swathed in an apparent sheet. A naked child, holding a wreath, stands just by her left knee. She holds a staff, that is, a long stick but not really a pole or something one could really belabor anyone with, and she does not appear to rest on it with any weight. She dallies with it, so to speak. Just to the child's left, is the major presence of the group, discounting, for the moment, the poet, and this is a man, or more accurately, a god, whose right arm reaches across his chest at shoulder height, to point with index finger at the poet's notebook or papers or text, which he has resting on his knee, his left hand securing them. The man or god's right arm is resting, close to the armpit, on a golden lyre, which catches the light (all figures and things are illumined by a strong frontal light coming from their right or, as one looks in, the viewer's left—a setting sun?). This figure has no clothing on the upper part of his body, but has a short skirt of crimson which breaks just above his knee as he sits. He wears a wreath, possibly of laurel, and his look is directed to the poet's pages. The poet, since this is *Inspiration of the Poet, L'Inspiration du poète, Die Eingebung,* has a remarkably unformed face and long hair, as have all figures in sight with degree depending on age and condition. He looks up, poised in some tentative thought, and is holding an instrument of writing, silver, which also catches the light. Just above him, to the viewer's left, poised between the god and the man, is a small baby, naked, with outstretched arms holding a great wreath as if he were about to encircle the neck of the poet therewith. The woman, the more she is observed, seems to be waiting for the god, as if he were shortly to be finished and they might go somewhere else together. Or else she waits for the poet? It seems to be her child, that is, the one standing close to her. He is also holding an object in his other hand, the one not occupied with the wreath, but it is not clearly discernible. There is a postmark which includes a section of the god's head, and then a sequence of six horizontal wavy lines to the right of it, moving across the image, but neither the printing nor date is legible. The god wears silver or possibly gold sandals, which also catch the light from the viewer's left. It is now clearly a sky, blue, which appears beyond them, far reaching clouds catching the fading sunset in tones primarily of orange and brownish grey. The poet's left foot is posed so that it seems to drag back of him, a curious crouch, in fact. Listening carefully, the viewer hears now a voice speaking. *Check it out. I'd like to tell you about something truly exciting.* It may be the god who speaks thus. *It's a soft little cup which adapts to you individually.* There is sadness, remembering. The words come from other times and the poet knows that *the twenty-first is tomorrow.* Also other people will speak. It is as if Poussin had anticipated these possibilities, and it is a lovely thought. "I send greetings with this card and the wish for a sustained and sustaining inspiration." The sun sets and all disperse, leaving the three trees they had chosen to sit by, for the accomplishment of their severally appointed ends.

•

Stopped at the intersection and asked to give directions, they cannot remember clearly if the house is below the one they are thinking of, or just above it, or on right side or left. They themselves have just come through the grove of cedars and are heading for the lights of the small city below them. They are a little surprised by the articulation of the questions because these people cannot be expected to speak English. The Dane, with them, laughs and says that he avoids the problem by living in a castle. He says that it is easy to find.

Romantic histories? Or fragile symbols of an uncertain light. It is not clear to them why the car has stopped so far from the town to ask such directions, or why it should be of them, so faintly apparent from the roadside where the car has been pulled over. There seems an invincible arrogance, a secular power, to the reason, whatever it may prove to be.

But there are two wings, two wings that go nowhere. To the house, or to the castle perhaps. No, it is a bird, that is silent and sad, the Dane says. There is no sound from the car as the people in it, not quite possible to see clearly, wait for further explanations. In case the terrible sun of the tropics shines for an instant, she wears sun glasses, a profound night of the eyes. This is the woman to the left of the driver, hooded figure, they now discern, with long talonlike fingers holding the wheel. The night prepares to fly from these depths of quiet objects. They think to move on but the immanent presence of those in the car will not let them. The lights below them appear to waver and flicker, and the city itself becomes inactual as they try to replace it. Without a look in their direction, the driver suggests it would be most helpful if they might come into the car, and go with it, until the house is found. Then they would be taken to whatever place they wished. He dictates, they realize, the mode, the custom, the domestic use of memory, and they are powerless to retrieve another purpose.

What a day it has been. Nights follow, one thinks. What a day after day after day, now, presently they are walking and talking about it, their strange lives. They have not as yet come to the car, already waiting for them, one thinks. The dog has found a resplendent bone in the garden but the castle is empty until evening, when the lamps are lit and men and women come into the great dining room for their food and water and ample conversations. The Dane laughs his great laugh and passes on the meat, the bread, the other things to be eaten. Sly, he uses the occasion also to fondle attractively the various women or men who attract his amorousness, since the night will wear on.

The car has by this time left the city. Hours earlier, it swung in the air, at the end of a magnificent crane used for unloading cargo, hooded in canvas, and was dropped, four wheels square, onto the dock. Four persons, undeterminable, but for the fact one seemed to be a woman, and a lovely one, go directly to the car, once it has been freed of its encumbrances, open its doors, get into it, and start, abruptly, its motor. Without further sign to any of those who observe them, they have driven off into the city's winding streets. They leave behind them the feeling of the day's fragments, years in conflict, and an indescribably solemn clamor. Those still watching suddenly put their hands, in apparent anguish, to their ears.

Backwards, they are turning the pages in their heads, looking for the place they had left off being there. The sight of

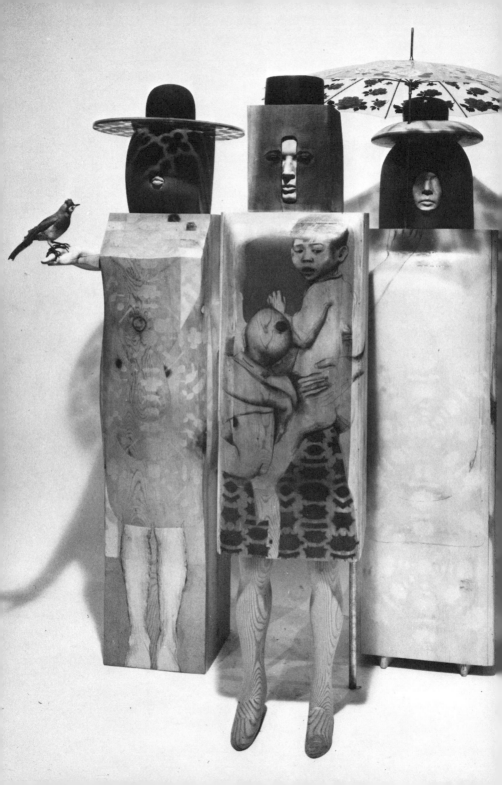

the woman has stilled them. They see the petrified flower, the antique bird, the lips so sensually and forever sealed. In the car the driver spins the wheel right, left, independent of direction. Although the woman sits directly next to him, her hands moving from time to time to his face, his hair, his leg, he makes no response. It is the limit of a hundred distinct possibilities, a retrogression to nothing, possibly, and they are fearful of breaking the profound silence or of provoking these angels of the tedious.

How wise to have the simple answer. The Dane is laughing insofar as the castle has fallen into his hands, kings and queens all. He is insolent but right, indefatigable position. All obey his ownership and subserve his underlying purpose, which is to use them one and all. The great halls resound to his pleasure, laughing, and night is turned into day with the merry-making. Only the great oaken beams supporting it all know the mystery of its diverse information. It is that wood is shaped by its maker, earth, water, or hands. Inside the walls, pinioned by the mortar's weight, the workmen look out through the cracks, sadly, at the lovely sight.

The Dane, in the car, longs for his castle. He makes shift to invite these new informants to come to it, not the house they have had in mind. He assures them of great and insistent provision, gives them all his heart in a flood of pain.

They think of love as they had known it, hands shaped as hearts, and held with inexpressibly tender containment. They think of mouths, opened, closed. Eyes and hands, with hair, fingers pointing them on. They think of sudden ambitions, regrets, plans, recognitions. Impossible Pegasus for impossible heroes, the car does not answer them but continues.

There is one way into the king, having at one time had a king, remembered. There are crowns, inextricably headed. Bearded figures in long gowns with boots of strict leather. There are places the people themselves will recall, summon back in fits of irritation, to have one word more. They want the car to stop since the house will not come to them, however fast or slow they approach it. The Dane is only their friend and the most helpless of them all. In the castle his bags sit unpacked by the bed he has never laid down upon. The defiant gesture, the inert adamancy, are history of the moment only, and fall back of them in the car's movement forward. There follow years and centuries, generation after generation. They push and pull, discreetly, hopefully, but to no avail.

Unity is the essence of all, the force which holds it all together. The woman extends her hands, her body, toward them, mockingly loving. Whether as mother or lover, she lures them to her own amusement.

Why do they fear. It will not hurt them. Why do they ask so tentatively. They will not be answered. Where do they think to go or to return to. They will not.

●

Back to back, these situations of *tortured sensibility*. Does that mean the sound of finger nails scraping a blackboard, the old proposal of sliding down razor blades on your heels, or simply the sharpened stick pushed into your eye, tongue cut out, penis slit, fingers crushed, both legs broken at the ankle. Coincident with consciousness is an ability not only to know things, but to recognize and anticipate *feelings,* even to propose them, the terror or pleasure in that act not-withstanding, so that the reality so engendered becomes the experience of the world entirely.

Angered, outraged, they got on the plane in Chicago. There was shaky agreement in London, but insistent flarings of temper and irritation. Friends put up with them, with him in particular, and at one point late at night in an alley re-trieved the garbage he drunkenly poured out of the cans standing along the edge of the street while also picking up the clothing his wife in rage pulled off to throw at him in rejection. Then Paris, exhausted, quieter, walking again with friends after a brief and confused lecture he had given at the Sorbonne, the lovely spaces and tones of the city, their hosts' argument relieving their own. And finally Italy, where they were to stay for a month at a villa in northern Italy on Lake Como, facing across to the Alps in late spring. They were met at the airport in Milan by a car and driver bearing the villa's insignia and then driven through flat city streets, then fields and increasingly winding roads to the villa itself, sitting above the town on a high promontory so that the intersection of two lakes met at its point. They were greeted by the director of the villa and his wife, introduced to those also in residence, some ten or eleven men and women, and taken to their rooms.

His own outrage was involved entirely with proposal, and with, he considered, what he had accomplished, their present situation being its latest condition. He loved her as he had assumed her to love him also, and he had been away, returning with the usual nervous hysteria and demand, to be, hopefully, comforted by her, his laundry seen to, and then he was off again, to make more money in a manner he found both egocentrically pleasing and hateful, by public lecture. They were to meet in Chicago at the airport. He remembered precisely the table they sat at, after he had asked her, obviously expecting no answer to confuse him, if she had fallen in love with anyone during his absence. When she answered, in her usual truth, that she had, but that it could not work, and that she continued to love him also, he was dumbstruck. A myriad of possible details, pruriently demanding, flooded his head. He insisted on facts, as he said, going over and over the dilemma of the information in his own increasingly drunken mind until they realized they had missed the flight to London. He called a friend and they went to his house, but the difficulty would not be eased, and they fought there too, himself falling and cutting one wrist on a glass that had been broken in their struggling together. The friend got them to a hospital where his wrist was sewn up by a contemptuous young doctor, without anesthetic, possibly to make him feel the ugliness he was exuding. The friend left and after some walking, they found a hotel still open and spent the night in a restless attempt to sleep.

He was at the villa ostensibly to write. Both realized that it was markedly difficult to be long alone with each other in that his obsessively recurrent questions brought them again and again to bitterly useless argument. Too, the privacy necessary to her own life was being battered by his attacks.

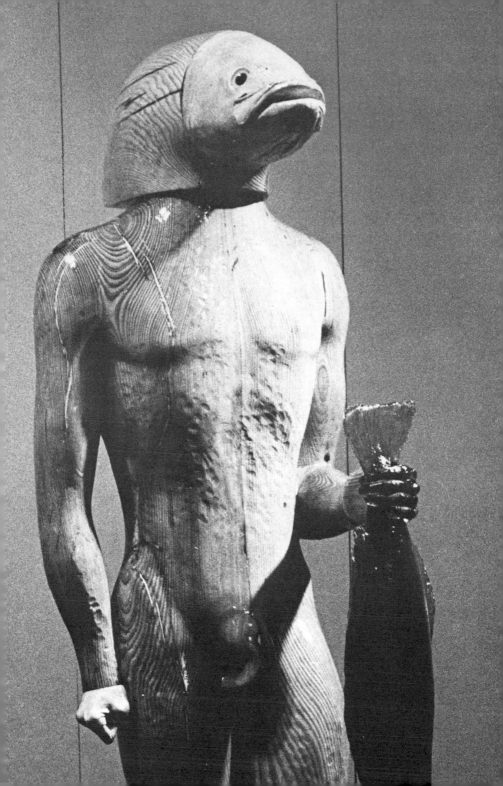

The alternatives were the other people, of course, but most were occupied during the day, either with their own work or with trips out into the surrounding country which he could not afford for his wife and himself. So he asked if it might be possible to have a small room apart from their suite given him for his own use.

At one point in the villa's history one of the militant Sforzas, who then owned it, designed a retreat for his monastic brother in the form of lovely gardens and walks through charming copses of trees. Small cells, or *casetas,* were erected at various points along the edges of the cliff for meditation, and it was one of these he was now given, in which to work. Its space was roughly six feet square, with large window extending almost to the floor overlooking the lake. It seemed a small tower, of stone, and delighted him entirely.

So each morning he would retire to the caseta, while she went on up the path to the ruins of a small castle on the very head of the hill which the villa occupied. This was encircled with a low wall of stone and again the view was impressive. At noon he would break off whatever he was doing and go up to join her, and both would wait for the appearance of two of the villa's servants, in white jackets, carrying a lunch for them in a wicker basket complete with fruit, wine and napkins. Sitting there, it was possible for him to let go of his resentment and to be with her in a way actual to the place itself.

He had come to Europe first as a young man, after the war, but only briefly and then only to England. His group was being repatriated and while they waited for other priorities to be respected, they sat in a small army camp close to Cardiff. That had acquainted him with the *oldness* of Europe, but it was a very faint sense. He had been with these people in a war, the most contemporary of realities, and continuing with them elsewhere did not lessen that impact of the present. After marriage, he returned to Europe with his family, and lived for two years near Aix in the south of France, then for about the same period in a small town in the Balearic Islands of Spain. His self-conscious use of either French or Spanish kept him from ever really being there as an actual person of the place, but the daily involvement of his family certainly made him common. Especially in France, when he went out into nearby woods to attempt to find wood for a fire, he had the feeling he was walking on ground that innumerable persons had also walked on, over and over, making a weight of time he had not thought of as possible. Human life he had begun to recognize as an accumulation of persistent, small gestures and acts, intensively recurrent in their need if not, finally, very much more than that. The *ideas* they delighted in, or suffered, however much they did affect the actuality of all, were nonetheless of a very small measure of possibility. Hunger or happiness, exhaustion or the security of home, both the measure and the vocabulary were extraordinarily simple.

At meals he considered, somewhat defensively, the facts of their company. He felt *nouveau,* an upstart, among them. He recognized their names as those of an eminent company. One, affable and in no wise condescending, had directed the Marshall Plan in Europe after the war. Another was a markedly famous journalist and spoke very easily of presidents and the worlds they are found in. A third, English, an accomplished historian, had been previous Vice Chancellor of Cambridge. To him he referred the poems of Basil Bunt-

ing, which the older man took off to his room with some interest. But himself, complacently angry and despairingly unable to regain a place familiar to him, was unwittingly awkward and almost hostile. In private he was both contemptuous and defensive. His wife, as love, had gone to hide her head among the stars.

A small brochure, given them on their arrival along with details of the times of meals and other daily activities, noted the history of the villa. Its first recorded possession was by Pliny the Elder, who had used it apparently as a farm and retreat from the hotter southland. Both Plinys make mention of it. Subsequently it was owned by the Sforzas previously mentioned, and must have remained for some time in their family. Leonardo da Vinci speaks of the view from that ruin where his wife and he ate lunch daily and, in his *Journals,* remarks that one may see the waterfall across the lake in the small town of Fiumetta. Stendhal had been a visitor, as had also Flaubert, and in modern times, as one says, Mussolini, fleeing for his life, had been apprehended as he was trying to reach it. It was finally purchased by the daughter and heir of a wealthy American whiskey manufacturer and then given by her to the foundation whose grantee he now was. The Kennedys had used it, for conferences, despite the irritation of its administrators. It went on and on.

One night, after a particularly nattering attack on her, his wife left their room, still in nightgown and robe, and went off through the interminable corridors and passageways to escape him. He thought to go after her, but at the door, looking out at the silence of the dark halls, he could not. Later she reappeared, smiling, to tell him that one of the eldest servants, an old man who worked as night watchman, had seen her and deferentially offered to follow with his lamp so that she might find her way. How simple the intrusion of factual needs upon affairs of conjecture and assumption.

As he sat in the caseta, sunlight flooding the window, the lake far below, what was so adamantly there to be written. "Sun bright,/ trees dark green,/ a little movement/ in the leaves." He could hear the sound of a small outboard motor on a boat below him, voices talking, laughing. Best that one's needs be simple because there seemed no true alternative to that condition. No one of those previously to have been here, not the farmer nor soldier nor monk nor artist nor writer nor dictator nor anyone at all, were more actual, after all. It came and then went. "Birds singing/ measure distance,/ intervals between/ echo silence."

•

$$\frac{2 \cdot 3 \cdot 1}{\text{Five}}$$

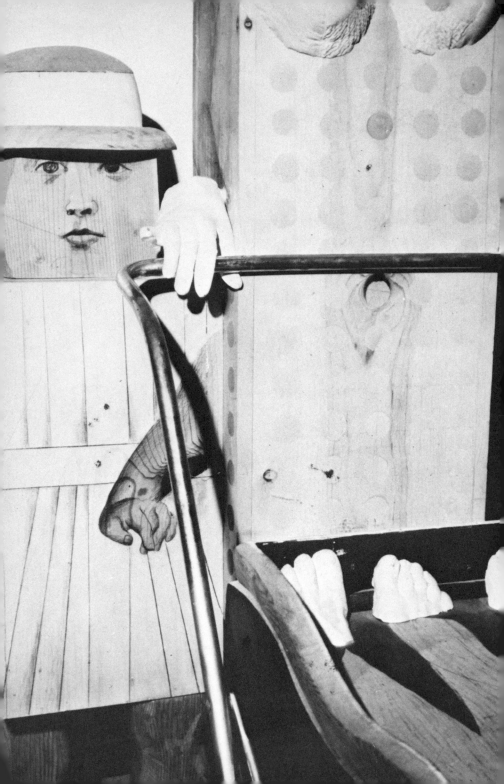

Waiting for the door to open, they think that Betty's teeth are equally present in Marjorie's mouth. They look the same, large, white, hard. The horse seizes upon the carrot in the small child's hand not because he is hungry, but because he has extraordinary teeth. Teeth work in the mastication of food in a manner mutually agreed upon by uppers and lowers insofar as these do meet, upon the jaw's being closed. Open or closed, the doorway itself stood empty although they waited still. His mother would often both delight and frighten him by popping forward the two plates of her false teeth, to make an extraordinary face. Most people know that George Washington's teeth were made of wood. Teeth is the plural of tooth in much the same manner as wives is the plural of wife, or *rooves* possibly means more than one roof, though it is entirely a situation of personal choice, depending on the person or persons involved with saying such things. People waiting in fixed circumstances of anticipation often find themselves committed to speaking in a manner frequently without interest.

Raise the roof, he said, biting his teeth in anger. He ground his teeth in his sleep. He had frequently a toothache. Dentists take care of teeth for payment and spend much of their waking hours looking into mouths. They wait for the door to open without apparent interest, knowing it will only be more teeth. Sometimes they are committed to pulling out teeth, no doubt feeling relief in getting rid of them. Young boys are often told that the vagina contains teeth. The tooth mother (*mater dentata*) is one of the significant guises of the great mother herself. Teeth are frequently hung around the neck in the form of a necklace. Dark spots on the teeth may signify caries or cavities in the tooth itself. People frequently make an inordinate sound chewing celery, a noise attributable to the action of the teeth. One may have buck teeth, a term possibly having to do with rabbits. Others have broken teeth, or possibly missing teeth, where some blow has caused the specific tooth to loosen and fall out. "I'll knock your teeth down your throat," is a phrase used to intimidate anticipated opponents in some muscular struggle.

"The rat has teeth," is the first line of a poem translated from the Chinese by Ezra Pound. "Habet dentes," is part of the phrase with which he was involved. I have a car and will drive you to Des Moines, says Betty. Marjorie notes the population of Des Moines is 209,000. Although neither has as yet come, they are close friends of the assembled people who wait for them with unabated interest.

What is anger that, when she at last arrives, Betty's teeth are knocked down her throat? Marjorie's mother has teeth and will not let her come. They have all gathered in a bus station while waiting to be driven to Des Moines. One of the more thoughtful of the group takes out a small volume of Ezra Pound's Chinese translations and begins reading the one about the rat's having teeth. It is well received by all who listen. Betty, tickled by the parallel reference, laughs through broken teeth. The door at last opens and those who come in realize they know none of those who are there. Where are we, is one of the first statements made by persons in both groups. The question, questions, hangs, hang, in the air.

One thinks the most distasteful of possible human practices is the knocking out of teeth on battle fields so as to possess the gold to be found in them. He can recall no instance of dentists' offices being burgled for the gold to be found in

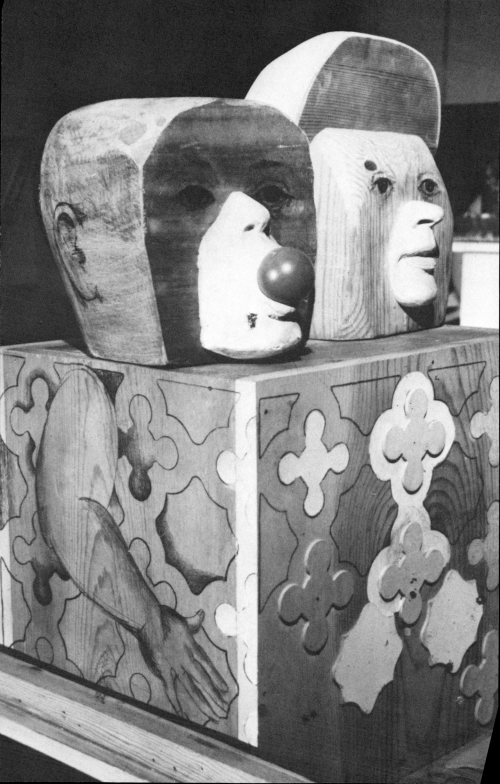

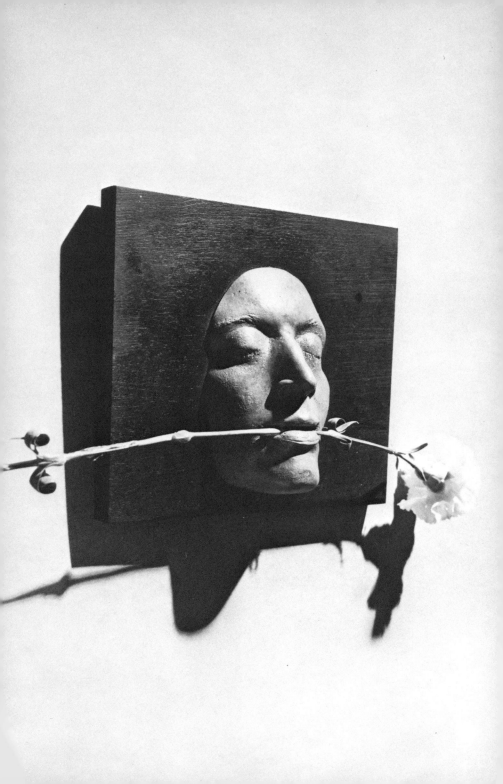

them in anticipation of using that metal for inlays. Nor is there clear sense of what happens to removed teeth, unless one is still a child. He dreams of the tooth fairy, come to reward him for letting his grandmother pull out the dangling front tooth. The tooth itself is under his pillow but the subsequent hand, reaching under there to possess it and leave the money in its place, moves with such assured stealth the sleeper has no consciousness of what is really going on.

One will never forget the large gold tooth hanging outside the office of the hero in a novel by Frank Norris, although one has never literally seen it. In like sense one tends to remember God, although he has not frequently been seen either. The mind has a power, like teeth, and immediately bites into what it has anticipated as prospective reality. One friend was a dentist for the mentally disturbed and recounted innumerable stories involved with teeth in sexual associations. The skulls of skeletons contain teeth more frequently than any other remnant of the clearly human condition, excepting the bone itself.

Teeth are permanent fingernails, that require no cutting. The blades of the harrow are often called teeth. Gears have teeth as do a great variety of fish. He wants to throw away his teeth in the anticipation of freedom. The sowing of the dragon's teeth resulted in the instant growth of formidable warriors, who attacked forthwith those who confronted them. The false teeth still kept in the drawer, although the actual owner had died, were subject of great interest to the young. Teeth are gall stones, in the mouth, with sharp edges. The teeth of the saw had been dulled by attempting to cut into metal. Some persons file their teeth, primarily for the appearance thus gained. Horses have their teeth filed to permit them to eat more comfortably. Who has not had his tooth removed by being sawed into four sections, and does not remember it? Steel teeth, despite rusting, might prove more convenient than wooden teeth, which would become soggy by constant immersion in the mouth itself.

The love bite, or nip, is practiced by animals and humans. The ear, especially, is seized upon. Betty's teeth were attractive, as were Marjorie's, but upon being hit in the mouth she realized that they were now gone. One forgets that walking into the teeth of the blizzard is an unfortunate circumstance. The police want teeth put into laws because they are hungry. Toot, toot. To sound a horn or whistle in short blasts. He showed his teeth, expecting trouble.

The door was a mouth without teeth. The broken windows of the vacant factory looked like teeth in a broken mouth. The teeth lying on the beach apparently belonged to no one. They could not remove the dog's teeth from the shoulder of the small victim. Remembering Betty and Marjorie, and going to Des Moines, is true. Getting one's teeth into it clears the head and the air.

•

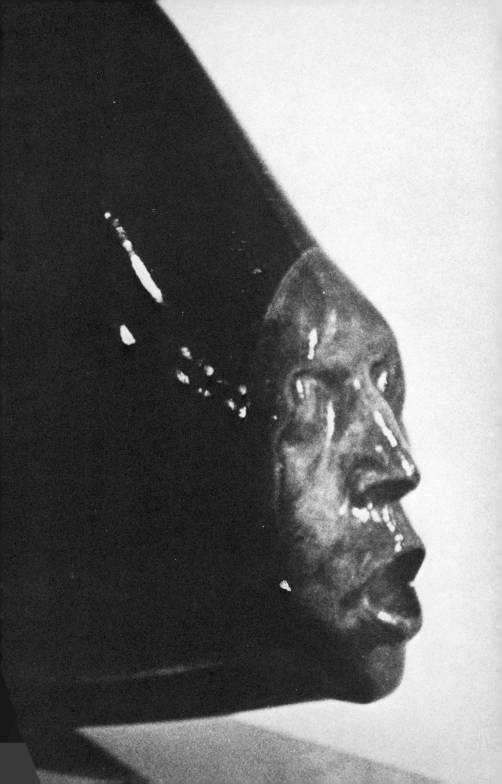

The stories keep coming back even if the people themselves are long gone. Memory seems to stay active no matter anyone really wants it that way, and the old *do you remember the time* number is a really heavy one. I went back last summer to see what the place looked like now, and I found they had moved the road from out in front of the stone wall, where it used to be, to even further out front, so that you can't even see that the house is there at all. The house itself and the barn and shed look much the same, but they have added some other buildings toward the back of the field, and it looks pretty settled in a way it never did when we were there.

Those days it seemed we would go the whole winter without much company at all, except for the few families that lived within a mile or so of us, up the road. When summer came, we were always pretty eager to have friends from the city come up and spend some time with us. One friend even took a job working in the woods, to help us keep the scene together. That was the summer we lived for the most part on chickens and blueberries since that was all we could get hold of. The garden hadn't come in yet and what we had canned ran out in the early spring. It was all an idea, in a way, but we were certainly serious and we were also young enough to bumble along without falling completely on our faces.

There was a lovely pool, up in the woods, formed by the river that came through part of our land, then angled off to make the lower boundary down by the railroad tracks where the large garden was. There was a smaller garden, for the kitchen, close to the house, but the big one was where we had the potatoes, corn, beans, all the vegetables we used primarily for canning. The pool used to get a lot of attention and it was well known to all our neighbors and even to the people in the outlying towns. One motel owner used to tell the people staying there, that they were free to use the pool, and that bothered us. In the summer the woods often got so dry that people smoking, or trying to make fires for cooking, could burn the whole woods down quicker than anyone could ever stop it. We tried to keep people out, just making it open to our neighbors, who knew what the risks were and were equally concerned, and still the other people kept coming. We even put up a big gate, anchored to posts that were sunk in cement, and somehow they got the whole thing out, posts, cement, and all. One time a travelling carnival, that had been in town over the weekend, chose our pool, or actually the road up to it, to dump all their garbage in. It took weeks to clean all that up.

So it was an idea, in mind, as to whether or not really to want people, any people, to come at all, much as we often did love them. Quail, and sometimes pheasant, would come to eat with the chickens, and that was a pleasure. During hunting season, when people were really careless and often drunk as well, we kept our dog close to home and sometimes other dogs, who had got on a scent, then lost themselves following it, would straggle into our yard. We'd check their tags, call the owners, usually local, and then they would come and get them. Our dog was a bitch and there was one particular old basset hound who would come, each year we lived there, and get himself stuck in the cat door, trying to get into the house. There we'd find him in the morning, wheezing away.

The people simplest to visit with were, in some ways, the various travelling salesmen that came through. By the time they had got to our place, they probably knew they weren't

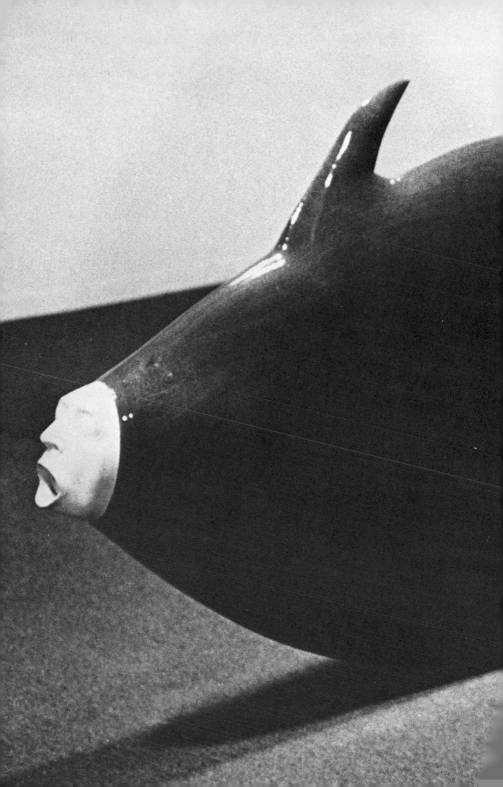

going to make any sales of any great amount, just that it was a poor part of the state and our place was obviously no exception. But it was lovely, especially in the summer, and they would come in anyhow, just to talk and look around a little. We would give them some coffee, or beer if we had it, and then we would all sit around telling whatever stories came to mind. There were two men selling siding for Johns Manville I especially remember, both of them sort of brash but good-natured and finally not really meaning to bother anyone. They tried to sell us some siding at first but when they realized we were broke, they just sat down and talked. They would joke about the siding itself, although it seemed as good as any other. One would take a piece of it, say, this is the strongest we got, never will break, then slap it down on his knee and it would shatter into a dozen pieces. That somehow seemed awful to us, just that we were the people who would usually be buying such stuff, and when the salesmen said, this is really strong, we found ourselves believing them more often than not. It was the idea again, that had really got hold of us. The same men had a sort of game they would play, to pass the time that must have got pretty boring, driving all those miles to all those old farms they hoped would buy some of their asbestos shingles. They came in all colors, some of them pretty loud for that part of the country, and so the salesmen would try to see what sort of wild color combinations they could get some unsuspecting farmer to let them put all over his house and barn. They would talk about a blue and orange one they had done over near St. Johnsbury, or else a pink and green one they had done down near Plymouth. Then they would laugh and we did too. It made us feel cheap but thankfully they weren't talking about our house and barn. It was a small blessing.

It was the idea of it all, that we could never get entirely clear. The salesmen were one small part of it. They were real in it, certainly. The farmers around us were, the people in town. One man we knew had never gone more than twenty-five miles from the place he was born. When we asked him one time if he'd like to drive down to Boston with us, his answer was he didn't know anybody there so he didn't see any point in going. A lot of the people were like that, even those who had gone into the army and been shipped to Germany or the Philippines. They just stayed there and when someone had gone away and then come back again, their usual greeting was something like, I haven't seen you around lately, and then whoever was talking would just pick up there as though the other person hadn't been gone more than a few days at most. That idea of people being in a place so completely we never could get to ourselves. We saw the people as moving in places and they apparently saw it the other way round.

There was one man I remember, who seemed a little different but no less of the place. We had geese that year and I let them range pretty much at will. One day a car stopped and this man got out to enquire if I had a gander for sale since he had several geese but no gander, but we got talking about geese, and then one thing and another, and I invited him in to meet my wife and have some coffee, and he accepted. I remember particularly his look, rather quiet and shy and a little withdrawn in that sense. He said he was the northern New Hampshire and Vermont representative for the International Correspondence School. He was also a deacon in his local church, over near St. Johnsbury. He was dressed neatly, in an old black suit, carefully so. He told us he was married to, as he put, a very sweet and very godly

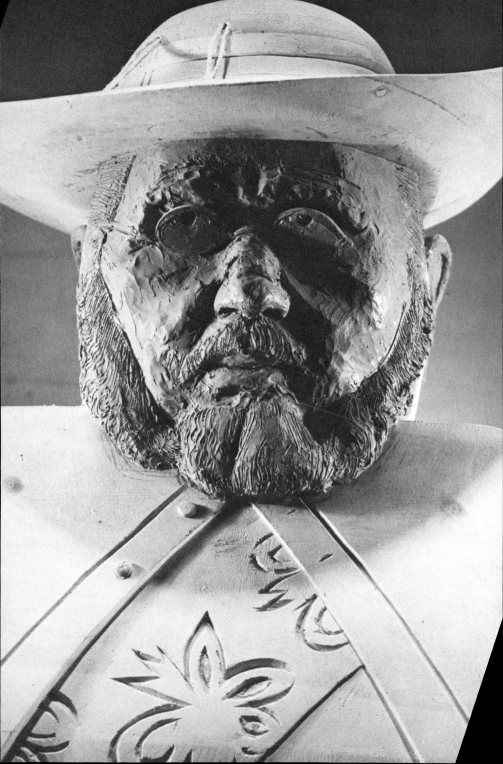

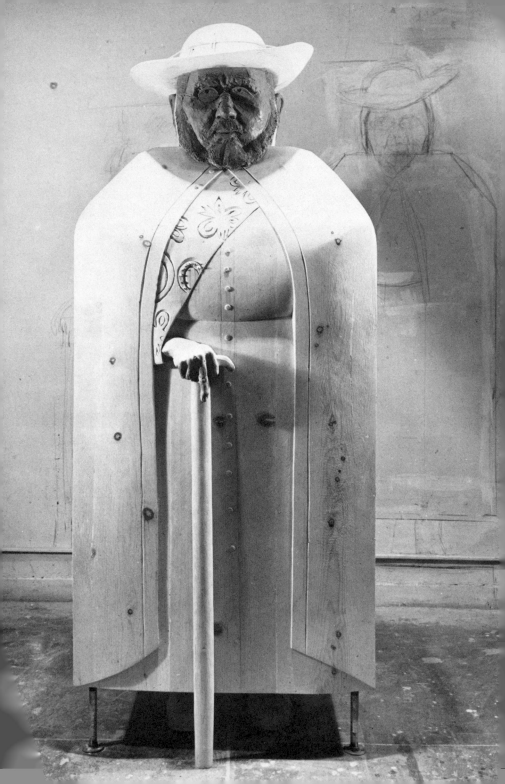

woman. He said she really had one aim in her life, and that was to make him happy and to do what he wanted her to. She never raised her voice nor let any of her own needs become more important than his. He said, in fact, that his only confusion in living with her was that he never really knew what she wanted or even if she wanted anything at all. He would try to please her at times, by bringing something back from one of his visits to get people to sign up for the correspondence courses, and she always liked it. It didn't seem to matter much what it was. It could be a flower he picked coming up the walk into the house or a new iron or even a new shawl or hat. She always liked it and said it was so good of him to think of her. He didn't make much money with his work and he knew that, and she never complained. One time, he was ashamed to say, he had lost his temper, he was so worried about what they might do next, they had no money, and she just said she knew it would be all right and that he would do just fine. He said he had hit her, and she never said a word or complained after that about it. He felt lonely at times just that he didn't feel he really knew what she wanted at all. It was almost too good, he said, her never wanting anything or saying anything, really, to him at all. He found he was driving a lot, and the car was not in very good shape, it was an old Pontiac, and he should keep it just for the business he had to, but at times he had to get out of the house. He loved her, she was his wife, but he wished she would talk to him and tell him what she really felt underneath.

His son worried him too, he said. He was a good boy, and a strong one, for thirteen, but he would forget things. H would start out walking to school and somehow never g there. School would be over and someone would come them that the boy hadn't been there and ask if he was sick. Sometimes it would even be dark before they could find him. He would just be sitting there, most often out in the woods by himself, and when they asked him what he was doing and why he hadn't gone to school, he couldn't answer them. All the boy would or could say was that he'd forgot.

•

Voices from the silence. Silencio immenso. Darkness falls from the air. When I show myself as I am, I return to reality. Vestida con mantos negros. Somewhere else, sometime. Walking in the rain.

When I show myself as I am, I return to reality. Piensa que el mundo es chiquito. Goes green, goes white. Weather falls out, raining. Applause at the edges. Seeing wind. When I show myself as I am, I return to reality. People should think of themselves when they live alone. Goes white.

Vestida con mantos negros, piensa que el mundo es chiquito. Thinks white. Falls from the air. Sees green, sees white. People should think of themselves when they live alone. Now I am not so sure. In the big city, you are your own best friend. I see you. Walks streets at night. Goes green, goes white.

I began to make self-portraits because working at night I had no other model. Thinks that the world is little. Weather walking, in rain. I used myself over and over again. Sees green. Passing people, goes forward, goes green, goes white. I would learn about myself. Y el corazon es immenso, laughing. Seeing tears, feeling edges. Pause of applause, in the big city. You are your own best friend.

I put things where they belong. I return to reality. People should think of themselves. Walks streets at night, working at night. I had no other model. I used myself over and over. I see you. In the big city. People should think of themselves. Goes green, goes white.

Turning. I like to make combinations that seem incongruous. I love you. I think they are coming. I wrote you last week. I want to sit here awhile by myself. I think it's better this way. I put things where they belong. A hand at the end of an arm. Goes green. Walks streets at night. Little world. She thinks the heart is big. Bigger. Biggest. I used myself over and over again. A mouth a little below the nose. Goes white.

Piensa que el mundo es chiquito. Small. Little. Not very much. I would learn about myself. I used myself. I show myself as I am. Goes green, goes white. The heart. Y el corazon es immenso. Large. Immense. Sees rain. A hand at the end of an arm.

I was very sad. I was very happy. I was thinking of rain, walking. People should think of themselves. I started doing something funny. I need a lot of affection. I return to reality. I had no other model. I used myself over and over. I put things where they belong. I show myself as I am. I started doing something funny so I would become happier. People I met were so depressing. And it worked. You are your own best friend. Vestida con mantos negros.

•

Postscript

"My death," said a certain ogre, "is far from here and hard to find, on the wide ocean. In that sea is an island, and on the island there grows a green oak, and beneath the oak is an iron chest, and in the chest is a small basket, and in the basket is a hare, and in the hare is a duck, and in the duck is an egg; and he who finds the egg and breaks it, kills me at the same time."

●

Photo Credits

In the listing of Marisol's work which follows, height, width and depth are listed in that order where all three are known, otherwise simply height followed by width. All works are "mixed media." The name of the photographer of each illustration is in parenthesis.

1·2·3

One

Baby Girl. 1963. 74 x 13 x 47". Albright-Knox Art Gallery, Buffalo, gift of Seymour Knox. (Jack Mitchell).

Baby Girl. (Jack Mitchell).

•

The Blacks. 1962. 78 x 26 x 7". Collection of Jonathan B. Larson, Minneapolis. (Jack Mitchell).

The Blacks. (Jack Mitchell).

The Blacks. (Jack Mitchell).

The Blacks. (Rudolf Burckhardt).

•

My Mother and Me. 1968. 73 x 56 x 40". Collection of the Artist, New York. (Jack Mitchell).

My Mother and Me. (Arno Hammacher).

The Bathers. 1961–62. 84 x 70 x 58". Collection of Mr. and Mrs. William Burden, New York. (Jack Mitchell).

The Bathers. (Jack Mitchell).

The Bathers. (Rudolf Burckhardt).

Baby Boy. 1962–63. 88 x 31 x 24". Collection of Mr. and Mrs. Albert A. List and Family, New York. (John Schiff).

•

Two

Untitled. 1961. 32 x 16 x 4″. Collection of Mrs. Eleanor Ward, New York. (John D. Schiff).

The Family. 1962. 3 x 66 x 12″. The Museum of Modern Art, New York, purchase. (Jack Mitchell).

The Family. (Jack Mitchell).

The Family. (John D. Schiff).

•

Portrait of Sidney Janis Selling a Portrait of Sidney Janis by Marisol by Marisol. 65 x 57 x 22″. The Museum of Modern Art, New York, Sidney and Harriet Janis Collection. (Jack Mitchell).

Portrait of Sidney Janis Selling a Portrait of Sidney Janis by Marisol by Marisol. (Mathews).

Dinner Date. 1963. 60″ high. Yale University Art Gallery, New Haven, promised gift of Susan Morse Hilles. (Eric Pollitzer).

The Party. 1965–66. 119 x 118 x 192″. Collection of Mr. and Mrs. Robert B. Mayer, Chicago. (Geoffrey Clements).

The Car. 1964. 47 x 121 x 36″. Museum Boymans-van Beuningen, Rotterdam. (Jack Mitchell).

From France. 1960. 54⅜ x 21¾″ deep. Unknown collection. (Rudolf Burckhardt).

•

The Generals. 1961–62. 87 x 28½ x 76″. Albright-Knox Art Gallery, Buffalo, gift of Seymour Knox. (Jack Mitchell).

The Generals. (Jack Mitchell).

•

Three

Henry. 1965. 67 x 31 x 16½". Collection of Mr. and Mrs. Brooks Barron, Detroit. (Jack Mitchell).

Guy. 1967–68. 84 x 48 x 12". Courtesy of The Sidney Janis Gallery, New York. (Jack Mitchell).

Mona Lisa. 1961–62. 66 x 11¾". Collection of Mrs. Babette Newburger, New York. (Jack Mitchell).

The Family. 1962–63. 79 x 45". Collection of Mr. and Mrs. Robert B. Mayer, Winnetka, Illinois. (Jack Mitchell).

John. 1961. 59 x 16 x 34". Harry N. Abrams Family Collection, New York. (Rudolf Burckhardt).

The Bicycle Riders. 1962. 68 x 66". Harry N. Abrams Family Collection, New York. (John D. Schiff).

•

The Band. 1963. 95 x 107 x 16". Collection of Mr. and Mrs. Leonard J. Horwich, Chicago. (Jack Mitchell).

The Band. (John D. Schiff).

•

The Party. (Geoffrey Clements).

The Party. (Geoffrey Clements).

The Party. (Geoffrey Clements).

The Party. (Geoffrey Clements).

•

Four

The Dealers. 1965–66. 74 x 74 x 41″. Museo de Arte Contemporaneo, Caracas. (Jack Mitchell).

The Dealers. (Jack Mitchell).

•

Women Sitting on a Mirror. 1965–66. 45 x 60 x 60″. Collection of Mr. and Mrs. Albert A. List and Family, New York. (Jack Mitchell).

Women Sitting on a Mirror. (Jack Mitchell).

Three Women with an Umbrella. 1965–66. 81 x 57 x 34″. Collection of Edwin Bergman, Chicago. (Jack Mitchell).

Untitled. 1965–66. 90 x 48 x 48″. Courtesy of The Dunkelman Gallery, Toronto. (Jack Mitchell).

•

The Fishman. 1973. 70 x 22 x 30″. Courtesy of The Sidney Janis Gallery, New York. (Irene Vilhar Studio).

The Fishman. (Irene Vilhar Studio).

The Fishman. (Irene Vilhar Studio).

Tea for Three. 1960. 64 x 22 x 27″. Collection of the Artist, New York. (Rudolf Burckhardt).

The Mayflower. 1961. 76 x 41½ x 10½″. Collection of Mr. and Mrs. Charles B. Benenson, New York. (Rudolf Burckhardt).

The Mayflower. (John D. Schiff).

•

2·3·1

Five

The Family. (Jack Mitchell).

The Family. (Jack Mitchell).

White Dreams. 1968. 9⅝ x 10¾ x 3½". Collection of Julius R. Wolf, New York. (Jack Mitchell).

Portrait of Betty. 1961. 15 x 11". Collection of Eleanor Ward, New York. (Soichi Sunami).

•

Green Fish. 1970. 18½ x 37 x 7½". Collection of the Artist, New York. (Irene Vilhar Studio).

Trigger Fish. 1970. 38 x 79 x 7". Courtesy of The Sidney Janis Gallery, New York. (Irene Vilhar Studio).

Zebrasoma. 1971. 65 x 78 x 15". Collection of Mrs. Richard Lombard, Rye, New York. (Irene Vilhar Studio).

Father Damien. 1968–69. Maquette for a Monument for The Capitol, Washington, D.C. and the Hawaiian State Capital Building. (John D. Schiff).

Father Damien. (John D. Schiff).

Sun Bathers II. 1967 89 x 38 x 40½". John Trouillard, Antwerp. (Jack Mitchell).

•

Women Learning. 1965–66. 67 x 86 x 41½". Collection of Edward Weiss, Chicago. (Geoffrey Clements).

Women Learning. (Geoffrey Clements).

•

Postscript

Six Women. 1965–66. 71 x 100 x 54″. Museum of Contemporary Art, Chicago. (Unknown photographer).

•